The Reason for Easter

Dan Halfman

Dan Halfman
2022

ISBN 978-1-63874-999-8 (hardcover)
ISBN 978-1-63874-998-1 (digital)

Christian Faith Publishing, Inc.
832 Park Avenue
Meadville, PA 16335
www.christianfaithpublishing.com

Printed in the United States of America

for the Gospel

Winter is over, it's turned into spring

The flowers are blooming, the birds start to sing

I can finally play outside without my big coat and boots

We play at the park on the ladders and shoots

When we go to the store, I see candy displays
Chocolate bunnies, eggs, jelly beans for days!
The Easter bunny is there, up on two legs
What's strange to me though, is rabbits don't lay eggs

Now this seems familiar, like I've been here before
Could Easter really be about something much more?
I remember at Christmas, I learned something new
Could I be missing the real reason for Easter too?

Again I turn to my parents, last time they were right
I think they'll know about this, I think they just might!

We sit down again, like we did last December

We open the Bible, and I start to remember

I remember we found answers, the scriptures were true

We learned Jesus was born to save me and you!

Jesus
ascends
into heaven

Jesus
appears
to many

Jesus
dies on
the cross

Jesus is
buried in
a tomb

Jesus
is crucified

Jesus is
resurrected

Jesus is
betrayed
and arrested

Jesus
goes on
trial

The Last
Supper

Jesus teaches,
heals the sick,
and performs
miracles

Jesus is
tempted
in the
wilderness

Jesus is
baptized

Jesus begins
his ministry

Jesus is in
the temple

Jesus
is born

11

But as it turns out, there's more to this story
A lot more would happen before his return to glory
Jesus grew up just like us, with one big exception
He never sinned. He lived life to perfection!

Even though he was good, not everyone was a fan
Some people hated him, that was part of God's plan
Jesus was betrayed, then arrested and tried,
Even though he was innocent, he was crucified!

15

Beaten and bloodied and nailed to a cross
Christ finally died, all seemed to be lost
They buried his body all alone in a tomb
If the story ends now, we are all doomed

But three days later, God's plan would unfold
Christ rose from the dead, just as He foretold!
Once His resurrected body began to draw breath
To Christ went the victory, He defeated death!

2 Corinthians 5:21

For our sake he made him to be sin who knew no sin,

so that in him we might become the righteousness of God.

But I still question the reason for this pain and despair
He did nothing wrong, it doesn't seem fair.
Then I remember what I've learned about sin
We all fall short, again and again

We break God's rules, on purpose or on a whim
We deserve punishment, certainly not him!
But God loves us so much, He's not done with us yet
Through mercy and grace, Christ paid *our* debt!

So because Jesus suffered and died on the cross,
Our sins are forgiven, His blood paid the cost
His resurrection finished it, wiped our sins clean
Brought us back to God, we are redeemed!

Clearly Easter is about so much more than I thought

More than eggs and candy, things that are bought

The reason for Easter is a free gift you can't see

Eternal life through Christ for all who believe!

About the Author

Dan Halfman is a Christian, a husband, and a father. He writes children's books that share the gospel in a way that both children and adults can relate to. After reading many classic children's books to his own kids, Dan was inspired to use this method to deliver biblical truths to young readers. Dan is also the author of the children's books *The Reason for Christmas* and *God's Love*. Lord willing, his books will help more people come to accept Jesus Christ as their savior. Dan is a physical therapist in Ankeny, Iowa, where he lives with his amazing wife and wonderful children.

CPSIA information can be obtained
at www.ICGtesting.com
Printed in the USA
BVHW022337250122
627171BV00002B/36